SWING TRADING MASTERCLASS

PROVEN TACTICS, TOOLS AND
PROFITABLE STRATEGIES

by Kenneth O'Neil

Copyright © 2019 Kenneth O'Neil
All rights reserved
ISBN: 9781799108832

© COPYRIGHT 2019 BY KENNETH O'NEIL

The following book is reproduced below with the goal of providing information that is as accurate and reliable as possible. Regardless, purchasing this book can be seen as consent to the fact that both the publisher and the author of this book are in no way experts on the topics discussed within and that any recommendations or suggestions that are made herein are for entertainment purposes only. Professionals should be consulted as needed prior to undertaking any of the actions endorsed herein.

This declaration is deemed fair and valid by both the American Bar Association and the Committee of Publishers Association and is legally binding throughout the United States. Furthermore, the transmission, duplication or reproduction of any of the following work including specific information will be considered an illegal act irrespective of whether it is done electronically or in print. This extends to creating a secondary or tertiary copy of the work or a recorded copy and is only allowed with express written consent from the Publisher. All additional rights reserved.

The information in the following pages is broadly considered to be a truthful and accurate account of facts and as such any inattention, use or misuse of the information in question by the reader will render any resulting actions solely under their purview. There are no scenarios in which the publisher or the original author of this work can be in any fashion deemed liable for any hardship or damages that may befall them after undertaking information described herein.

Additionally, the information in the following pages is intended only for informational purposes and should thus be thought of as universal. As befitting its nature, it is presented without assurance regarding its prolonged validity or interim quality. Trademarks that are mentioned are done without written consent and can in no way be considered an endorsement from the trademark holder.

A Technical Note

Given that some important swing trading education elements are advised to be studied in color, I have decided to offer you a FREE electronic copy of this book in **color**. To prevent unauthorized access to the download link through Amazon book previews, I have placed it in the very end of the book.

Thank you!

Best,
Kenneth

TABLE OF CONTENTS

INTRODUCTION - WHY SWING TRADING? 7
    Swing trading vs. day trading 11
    How to leverage small gains over time 13

CHAPTER 1 - UNDERSTANDING SWING TRADING: HOW DOES IT WORK? 15
    Building a Foundational Investment Strategy 15
    Support and Resistance 21
    Trading Fibonacci Retracements 25
        More on Fibonacci 28
    Building a Plan 33

CHAPTER 2 - SWING TRADING STRATEGIES 37
    Candlestick Charts 37
    Reading a Candlestick 40
    Bulls vs. Bears 42
    Basic Candlestick Patterns 43
    More Complex Patterns 47

 How to Trade Candlestick Patterns 56

 Moving Averages 59

 Building Blocks 63

 More Trading Patterns 70

CHAPTER 3 - PRACTICAL TIPS AND TRICKS **73**

 Rules 73

 Backtest 81

 Costs of Trading 85

 Goals 89

CONCLUSION **92**

APPENDIX - GLOSSARY OF SWING TRADING TERMS

.... 95

INTRODUCTION

WHY SWING TRADING?

Billions of dollars in commodities, currencies, stocks, and bonds are traded around the globe not just every day, but every hour. Is there money to be made in the margins of those transactions? The answer a resounding **YES!**

That is, of course, the easy part, identifying the opportunity. The second question, of *how to exploit it*, is decidedly more complicated. It is, however, not insurmountable, as this book will identify. The steps involved when entering the trading world are not difficult, but they do require careful application and discipline. As you move through the chapters of this book, I hope that you will discover the ease with which you can become a successful trader.

So, why *swing trade* as opposed to *day trade*? There are a number of reasons. For one thing, you hold stocks overnight and avoid having to establish a day trade account that requires a $25,000 cash investment. Furthermore, you can make money part-time from investing and easily hold a 9-5 job. And if you do want to eventually transition to full-time trading, swing trading allows you to find a happy medium; you don't have to go all in right away.

Or more simply, you may just not want to hold long positions, and instead, prefer to capture a swing over a few days or a week. Although whatever the scenario, I strongly advise not to trade with capital that you *cannot afford to lose*, especially when starting out. Plan for worst-case scenarios when starting out and be pleasantly surprised when trades turn to profits. On a much more positive note, it does not take a lot of capital to start swing trading, as I will demonstrate.

Note, swing trading, while in some ways similar to day trading, does have significant differences, differences that work in favor of the *part-time trader*. As stated above, trades in a variety of industries, across a variety of trade vehicles, take place every hour of the day, 24 hours a day, around the globe. Day traders hold positions for hours, sometimes minutes, in an attempt to capitalize on brief swings in the market. This, of course, requires a full-time commitment (in some cases up to 80 hours a week) to realize any success.

The goal of *swing trading* is to identify the overall trend in any given market (i.e., bond, stocks, and commodities) and capture gains with swing trading within the trend that the market is developing. This requires holding security or commodity (although more often than not, swing trading deals in securities) for days, sometimes weeks.

Yes, more than likely, there will be small fluctuations in the market in that period, but if you can successfully identify the market direction; your gains will likely be *greater* than a comparable day trader making multiple trades in the same period.

Finally, having taught many beginning traders, I can say that swing trading, especially for the novice investor, is less risky and definitely more approachable.

In the following chapters, you will learn how to analyze and identify those trends and various investment strategies, providing you with more conservative options as well as higher risk and greater reward opportunities. I will show you how to get started, how to do practice trades, and demonstrate the proven methods, already in use by thousands of investors, to successfully invest and build wealth.

Swing trading is **not** a *get-rich-quick* scheme; it is a proven investment technique that, with patience, can lead to reliable long-term returns. As we move through the following chapters and unveil how you can develop your swing trading acumen, it should go without saying that *patience is a virtue*.

How many times have you read of novice investors selling off their equities as fast as they can at the first sign of a downward trend? Experienced, savvy investors know that every market presents an opportunity, and they look to exploit that opportunity while others lose their heads (and profits).

That said, I welcome new and experienced investors to swing trading, and congratulate you on taking this step in wealth creation.

Swing trading vs. day trading

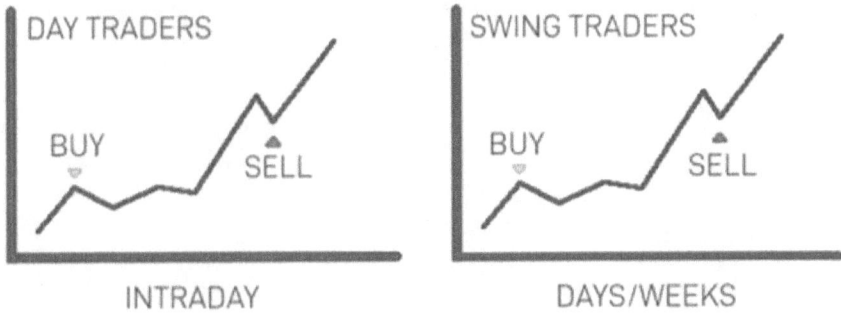

We touched briefly on the advantages of swing trading over day trading, but it's worth returning to this subject, as the following strategies may sound similar.

Probably the single greatest factor that differentiates swing trading from day trading is a barrier to entry. **FINRA** (*Financial Industry Regulatory Authority*) rules state that the term *'pattern day trader'* day trades (buys then sells or sells short then buys the same security on the same day) four or more times in five business days, provided that the number of day trades is more than six percent of the customer's total trading activity for that same five-day period, then a pattern day trader must maintain a minimum equity of $25,000 on any day that the customer day trades. Furthermore, the required minimum equity must be in the account before any day-trading activities. If the account falls below the $25,000 requirement, the pattern day trader will not be permitted to day trade until the account is restored to the $25,000 minimum equity level. That is a far higher bar to enter than a typical swing trader. Even a very minimal investment, as low as $500, is enough to establish a brokerage account and begin swing trading.

Based on the above requirement, you may have surmised (correctly) that swing trading is far easier to learn than day trading, which requires (to be done successfully) the ability to read complicated financial charts and trade on those charts within minutes.

Whereas with swing trading, using stop losses and profit targets, you can manage your account with far less stress (and with experience more efficiently). You do not have to be glued to your monitor for hours on end, babysitting your trade, and looking for your exit point. Day trading is a huge time commitment. Day traders can change their positions in a minute, and certainly, trading positions of fifteen minutes or less are very common. This means that you must constantly be monitoring your position.

With swing trading, you have a chance to breathe, you need to monitor your trades, and make sure you're in a favorable position, but obviously not with the intensity and stress of day trading. Also, commissions are lower on swing trading, since you will not be making multiple trades per day, which increases your spread on any given trade.

Best of all, in the end, you should be able to realize greater profits through swing trading, as letting your trades run longer and having greater flexibility should maximize your profits on a successful trade. Both can be profitable but swing trading allows for more profitability per trade, all other things being equal. Day traders need to exercise far more trades to realize the same profits. Do you want to make one or two trades a week or ten trades a day? For some, it is the latter, simply because that has become the technique they've developed, but for the vast majority of investors, this is simply not the case.

Although there certainly is a place for day trading, and if you have the time and the dedication to put towards it, it can be a profitable venture. Swing trading though is the best option for those who want to trade profitably without devoting their entire lives to it.

How to leverage small gains over time

Taking small positions allows you to be more nimble. Position traders usually like to achieve a twenty to twenty-five percent profit on trades. As a swing trader, you should strive to achieve five to ten percent profit on trades. While tiny, if you can do that on a consistent basis over multiple trades, you can achieve, over time, *significant investment returns*. This is the growing attraction of swing trading since aiming low and small positions allows you to take advantage of movement in the market institutional or large position traders cannot.

While swing trading is not trend-following per se, identifying trends does help us find entry points for investing. Whether it is the upswing or downswing, the beginning of that swing is our entry point. This usually means minor trend reversals of the overall trend. In other words, *buy on dips, sell on peaks*. So, for example, a price pulls back when buyers take a breath and ease off on the stock, otherwise, trending up will be an entry point on the anticipation of the stock continuing its upward trend.

CHAPTER 1

Understanding Swing Trading: How Does It Work?

Building a Foundational Investment Strategy

Let me now go a little deeper into the world of swing trading. All investing begins with careful analysis (or should at any rate). There are basic trend principles we can look at to develop a baseline, and from there, take in more factors to further develop our probabilities in making a profitable trade.

To start with, we have the *Pareto Analysis* or *Pareto Principle*, widely known as the *80/20 rule*. This rule is based on the observation that eighty percent of activity is generated by twenty percent of people. Originally put forward by an Italian economist, *Wilfredo Pareto*, who learned that 20% of people owned 80% of land in Italy. After further research and analysis, he discovered the country's wealth distribution as a whole followed the same pattern.

As more research was done on the Pareto Principle, over the decades, economists came to realize how applicable the 80/20 rule was to capital markets and trading. Without delving too deeply into this basic law of investing, we will boil it down to its basics. Which is: twenty percent of your entire efforts will result in eighty percent of your results. With this in mind, you know that most of your efforts will result in negligible losses or gains. Take this rule as part of your foundation, and let it reinforce in your mind the need for patience and discipline when investing.

Generally, you can count on *emotional responses* to create market movement. Greed, fear, and uncertainty are the three dominant emotions that can influence even experienced traders. When it comes to short-term price aberrations, almost all can be attributed to those emotions affecting buying and selling decisions. To be successful as a swing trader, you must ignore the tendency to react emotionally to price movement and use logic to take advantage of market overreaction. When prices rise quickly, the overall investing market tends to act out of *greed*, buying to get in on the anticipated profits. But you do not need to have that instant reaction. Yes, let their greed drive the market, and then try to take advantage of that.

As a swing trader, I am always looking for price action. Over any period and over any market, you should ideally develop a set of rules to classify price movement as either trending or range bound. Range bound or stock (or whatever you're following) has peaks and valleys, with no real losses or gains as opposed to up or downtrends.

That's a basic, and it does depend on the time frame. There are various ways to define what a trend is such as *Simple Moving Averages* (SMA), *higher highs* or *lower lows* against absolute momentum, which is the emotional traders either buying into the market late or selling off late as they try to stem losses.

Take the uptrend. Within several days of an uptrend, there will be pullbacks. So, how to capture a profitable trade? Trends have the principle of persisting in its trend. Keep in mind though that works both ways, and does include range bound patterns. If the trend is peaks and valleys, then it will tend to follow that trend and stay range bound.

We've talked about foundational strategies, so let's look at some basic rules to swing trading successfully. The biggest rule is to *go with the trend*. While that may seem contradictory to the previous statement of greed, it is not. Watch the trend, understand what's driving it, and look for a profitable entry point. Very few people succeed as contrarian investors. Trends mean the market is not acting randomly. For example, the bull market of late 2016 to late 2018, if you had been investing on every price pullback on the Dow or S&P average in that period, you would have been following the trend and taking advantage of dips at points of *price resistance* (more on that later). And if you had done that, well then, it's unlikely you would be reading this book, as you would be a very successful trader.

However, you *are* reading this book, so where will the next price trend take us? Remember, with swing trading; the same profitable trades can be made on a downwards trade as stocks make points of price support before they continue to trend downwards. What we don't want is a *dead market*. If we have no movement up or down, we have no swing to capitalize on. Trying to swing trade in a dead market is like trying to drive a Ferrari in a traffic jam. It doesn't matter how good you are, you're still going nowhere.

Times to avoid trading are just previous to holidays for exactly this reason. At other times, a way to establish if a market is dead is to check the trading volume for the previous five sessions and see if the average trading volume is roughly equal.

Although we will go further into various investment vehicles in later chapters, it should be noted that for novice investors, your most consistent option will be *large-cap stocks*. Large-cap stocks make up over ninety percent of equities listed on North American exchanges. They are the most approachable from an analytic approach, as they are the most transparent to investors, and there is a great deal of free information available regarding these stocks. This will simplify your initial research, and as you develop a trading strategy, help you find an entry point with limited experience.

The other advantage of this is the more exotic or rare the investment vehicle, the greater the spread will be between the bid and offer. Some books will advise novice swing traders only to trade the 'long side,' i.e., the upward trend. This is <u>not</u> one of those books. As I have already noted, as long as you trade logically, and keep emotions in check, you should be able to trade the 'short side' (downwards trend) just as easily. Ignoring short side trades will very likely cause you to miss out on valuable opportunities. Please, remember that markets historically drop three times faster than they rise (because fear is a stronger emotion than greed). However, as we noted, market movement is what you want, so take advantage of it, there is no reason you can't be successful trading on a downward trend.

One way to identify trends is to track stocks in the same industry group. Stocks in the same industry group tend to correlate to each other over the market as a whole. If one tech stock is rising, but the market as a whole is flat, other tech stocks will also be outperforming the market. The same correlation holds for commodities and currency trading. So learn the correlation between assets and markets. This does not mean *'invest in tech as a whole'* if a major tech company is rising. That is not the lesson to learn here. If investing in a sector increases your exposure, don't do it.

Find the best performing stock or asset in a given sector. There are many components to consider when you are going to swing trade. Previously, we mentioned large-cap stocks as an asset to focus on. However, more experienced traders or traders with related professional experience may prefer *commodities*. Or maybe you are more inclined towards *currency trading* on Forex (a subject we will cover in a later chapter). Whatever the investment vehicle, my advice is to focus on <u>one</u> asset class, as otherwise you will become far too stretched trying to analyze and track trades across multiple asset classes. And again, large cap stocks will be the most accessible assets starting out, with little to no experience.

Once you have determined your asset class, your next step is to determine what your *trade set up* will be, i.e. a specific set of rules in which you are going to trade by. You have to determine what your initial *entry point signal* will be, and what your initial *stop/loss* will be in all cases, what your *exit* will be, and how much *capital you are willing to risk*. It would be a good idea to have these fundamentals written out in advance to avoid emotional reactions. Make it precise, not 'I'm going to risk $1,000.'

SUPPORT AND RESISTANCE

Before we go further into technical analysis and chart reading, we need to consider more market fundamentals namely *support* and *resistance*. These are critical points because this is where markets take a breather. We know price does continue in a straight line, it pushes up, and it thrusts down. Many fields of analysis will tell us where prices are going, but where is the next rung on the ladder?

Support and resistance give us entry and exit points, and why they are crucial pieces of information. As you may have surmised, the area on the chart where a price has a hard time going through is *resistance*. Stopping a price from dropping under a specific point is where *support* levels come in. Resistance and support are the ceilings and floors of the market; however, that does not mean price cannot breakthrough either. It is much easier to choose when to close and open trades when you have the knowledge to where these certain levels lie.

Your question no doubt then is *how can we locate these prices*, to begin with? It's very important to understand these concepts because there are many different tools or methods to project price resistance and support levels, and the levels themselves can be constantly reframed.

Knowing how to identify support and resistance will be a major factor in reducing losses as well as locking in profits. More specifically, it is possible for resistance and support to have several applications and can be recognized in countless ways. Traders can utilize resistance and support identification for handling risk in their trading strategy. Traders can also use resistance and support to rank enter positions and market conditions.

Defining support and resistance can be confusing to some, as they are not so many opposites, as two sides of the same coin. A better way to describe them is the elevator analogy. As you ride an elevator up, the floor of the elevator supports you as you *'break'* through the ceiling above, then that floor that was a resistance level now becomes the new support level, and so on as you rise. Then the entire concept is reversed coming down. You're constantly breaking through ceilings going either way, with resistance levels constantly changing to support as the price rises and vice versa.

When discoursing in the setting of the stock market, the defining idea of support and resistance is simple. It describes where the *law of demand and supply* come into the picture or the stages at which sellers and buyers come into the market. Discrepancies in demand and supply create resistance and support levels.

So, imagine you have a bunch of buyers. Let's say, for the sake of illustration, you're at a *cattle market* and have a *1,000 head* of cattle to sell. You tell the auctioneer to set the price at $63, and you sell a few heads of cattle at that price. So the price rises to $63.10, but there's no market at that price, and it drops back to $63.

That means $63 is your support level, you sell a few more cattle, and buyer demand goes up, so you go to $63.10 again and find a buyer, and go to $63.20, buyer, $63.30, buyer, then $63.40, and there are no buyers, now you have found your next level of resistance.

For other potential buyers who missed the first cattle auction, they may have heard $63.30 was the price, so that becomes in their minds the best price. But that only tells half the story. They may know the price, but not the *number of buyers*. Therefore, *volume* is the other critical component in determining resistance and support.

The more intense the selling or buying is at resistance and support levels, the signal being given becomes more significant. Price resistance and support come in many forms, panic sell-offs or blow off tops—can put bottoms and tops into the markets and mark significant resistance or support levels. Where the forces of demand and supply meet, resistance and support signify key junctures. Prices are determined by demand (going up) and excessive supply (going down) in the financial markets. With bearish trends, supply is synonymous. With bullish, demand is synonymous. Throughout this book, these terms are utilized correspondently. Also, when demand and supply are approximately equivalent, as bulls and bears fight for control, there is a sideward movement on the prices.

TRADING FIBONACCI RETRACEMENTS

Sometimes, support and resistance appear as *retracements*, which are short-term price corrections during an overall larger upward or downward trend. What's key here is that they are temporary price reversals and do not represent an indication of the larger trend, i.e., they are not a trend reversal. Finding and trading retracements are used for short-term trades; so clearly, they have value for swing traders if you can successfully track them.

Their main benefit is that they provide an opportunity to enter the original trend at a better price, before the continuation of the trend. If they are not a reversal of the trend, then why do retracements occur? Let's use a large upwards trend as an example, as buying pushes an asset's price upwards it, in turn, attracts additional buyers. At a certain point, those early buyers will take their profits, which will result in a suspension of upward momentum. But the sell-off does not reverse the overall trend, as many buyers who came to the market late will continue to hang on, resulting in only a short price pullback.

When looking for a possible retracement entry point, look for an asset in a strong upwards or downwards trend, and ideally, enter the market right after a pullback has occurred (in an uptrend). If tracking a strong downward trend you want to sell rallies, that is bought on the downtrend, and sell as the asset briefly rallies (it is easier to trade retracements on an uptrend, as it's harder to predict the peak of the rally on a downtrend).

That said, how do we know *when* a price pullback will occur?

This is where *Fibonacci retracements* come in. If you want your chart to have Fibonacci retracements applied to it, looking for both the low and high swing of a given time frame is needed. Let's say twenty days for this example. The swing high is the highest point the asset has reached in that time frame (not highest close). Likewise, the swing low is the lowest point in the same time frame. Draw a line between the swing low and swing high.

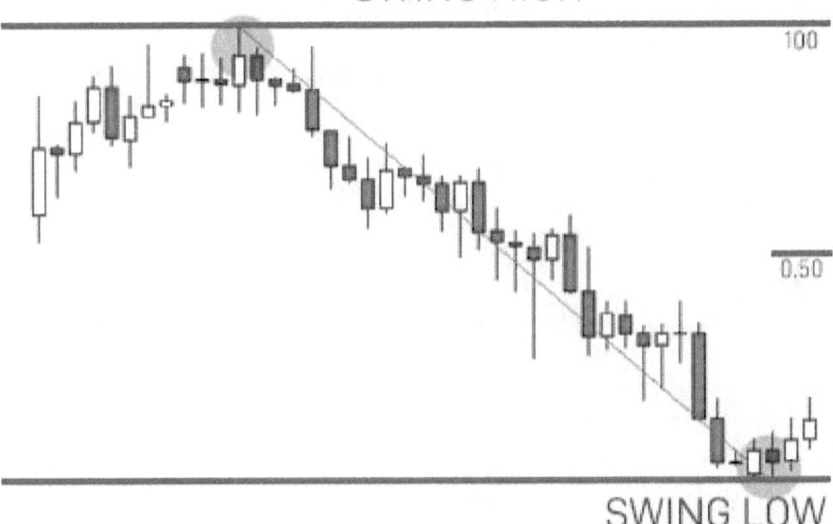

The rule of thumb is Fibonacci retracements occur at approximately fifty percent of the swing high point (there are complex mathematical formulas for predicting Fibonacci retracements that are out of the scope of this book. However, the rule of thumb here is sound).

More on Fibonacci

Fibonacci is named for its discoverer, *Leonardo Bonacci* (better known as *Fibonacci*, short for *"son of Bonacci"*), a thirteenth-century mathematician. It is sometimes called as the *Golden Mean* because its ratio can be found throughout nature, and it is also a very popular trading technique. That said, many experienced traders are often skeptical about the exact values, so it's worth going into a little more detail to understand the debate.

As we noted, Fibonacci works in any market, including Forex and stock, which, in fact, react easily to Fibonacci numbers and levels. Fibonacci trading involves knowing *when* and *where* the market reverses in order for it to keep moving.

As we have explained, in Fibonacci trading, the most significant thing is that the Fibonacci levels act as resistance and support. Yet, if you ask why Fibonacci Forex and

Fibonacci stock markets work, the true answer is *we don't know*, which is likely why some professional traders remain doubtful about its utility.

Fibonacci numbers can be applied to anything from the smallest to the biggest, and maybe unimaginable, aspects. It can be applied to the strands of our DNA or any other microscopic materials. You can also apply this in knowing how far the hands, ears, eyes, and such to one another. Even our solar system's planets and their distances can also be determined. Another example is the pathways of the stars in the universe and its various distances. The *Golden Mean* can work to any of these and to some other things. And finally, and more applicable to our needs, Fibonacci sequence is seen in the prices of the inner currencies and their down and up movements.

As a trader, all you need to know are the key percentages in Fibonacci retracements. Before trends continue in their original path, they tend to retrace which is represented by certain percentages. These levels of percentages can be marked by the traders the moment the retrace starts. They can be marked as a percentage of the distance of the trend (a slightly more complex reading of the 50 percent rule of thumb). At these levels, possible reversals should be anticipated. This can appear as another type of resistance and support.

78.6, 61.8, 50.0, 38.2, and *23.6* are the key percentages you should know. Why do we trust Fibonacci sequence if we don't wholly understand it? Specific mathematical relationships are where the Fibonacci trading is based. Ratios between numbers in a series are how they are expressed.

Prior moves are also retraced by these trends as found by the traders. They are according to ratios and are shown in the listed key percentages. Let's make the finished downtrend an example. After recovering 78.6%, 61.8%, 50%, 38.2%, or 23.6% of the previous downtrend, it tends to reverse or pause as it is retracing the downtrend and is moving higher.

Out of those, the three *most important Fibonacci levels* (often referred to as 'Fib levels') you should know, and keep in the back of your head are, *38.2, 50.0,* and *61.8*. As with the 50 percent rule, the movement of future prices - whether they will reverse or stall - can be better predicted by the traders. In order to do this, a line is drawn showing the percentage of the trend's previous retracements on the charts.

As I mentioned before, the real reason why trends seem to reverse or pause after they have recovered the previous trend's percentages is still not clear. Some might say it's related to mass psychology, since they represent a typical trader's psychological reaction to price changes. Ultimately, I suggest to compare the Fibonacci with electricity. We may not understand how these numbers actually work, but we still use them. Since they have become a widely watched and accepted indicator of support/resistance, that has become their proof that it works.

A degree of self-fulfilling prophecy has been created since people have now watched and accepted the Fib, like with other technical indicators. That being said, the anticipation of the price movements has taken advantage of the usefulness of the Fibonacci even more.

How the Fibonacci works can be seen in this illustration in a trading scenario. Look closely on the following chart:

Fibonacci trading in action can be seen in this example. In order to indicate the areas of resistance and support, horizontal lines are used by the Fibonacci retracements. First, the low/high of the chart given should be located. And then, that's when they can be calculated next.

Next is drawing five lines as follows:

1. The 1st line represents the high at 100 percent
2. The 2nd line at 61.8 percent
3. The 3rd line at 50 percent
4. The 4th line at 38.2 percent, and
5. The 5th line represents the low at 0 percent.

The new levels of resistance and support are often near or at these lines after an important movement of the price, either down or up.

Those are Fibonacci retracements; there are also *Fibonacci arcs*. These are similar and like Fibonacci retracements, although used in a different way (I mention them here mainly, so you are aware of them). You begin with finding the high/low on a chart for a given time frame. Then with a compass-like movement (as you might remember from your high school geometry class), three curved lines are drawn at the 38.2, 50.0, and 61.8 percentage points from the desired point on your chart.

There are also Fibonacci *fans* and Fibonacci *time zones* (which use vertical lines and different sequencing numbers). However, to go into the complexities of all these would require their book. For your purposes as a swing trader, remember that Fibonacci ratios are not meant to define the exact timing of your market exit or entry. They should rather be used in the estimation of resistance and support, which are crucial for successful swing trading. Many traders prefer a combination of Fibonacci arcs and other resistance indicators. Others use Fibonacci retracements in their technical analysis, which is my recommendation. Add these techniques to your tool belt, so you have a better comprehension of what the market is doing, and where you might initiate successful trades.

Building a Plan

- Firstly, you need to *know and standardize your rules*. What win/loss ratios, and how much risk per trade can you accept?
- You need to look at the basics, such as, can you afford to trade an asset? Perhaps, the stop loss might be too close. Position size has to be considered when looking at asset classes; if a stock is trading at $1,000, then your position may not be large enough to make it worthwhile. You

really have to know when to push the trade aside. Find the assets that fit your trading rules.
- There are many time frames in swing trading; usually, a two-day min to the thirty-day max is a sound time frame to keep your trades within.
- One of the key attributes of swing trading is to look out at the beginnings of a new swing. Often, these are very visually apparent. But you don't have to trade every entry point. Look to your rules to establish if a potential swing is a worthwhile trade.
- A good way to track your performance is to give yourself a set number of trades throughout a month. The reason for this is a good run in trading can quickly turn south even for the most experienced trader, and can easily turn into a two-month binge of self-destruction, and erase any gains you may have made, as you start to make trades to try to turn your 'luck' again.
- Never rely on luck for trading. Yes, sometimes, luck will play a factor, accept it and move on. Set the number of trades you will make in say, a month; five being a good number for that time frame. This will help instill market discipline and give you a reliable metric to base your performance on.
- What are key performance metrics you should track? Certainly, profit and loss are the most important,

although it is advisable to have at least one other metric. The ratio of profitable trades to losing trades is a simple measure to calculate your month to month performance. Say, for example, over a ten trade cycle, you profit $1,500 over $500 in losses, giving you a profit ratio of 3R, or three times more profitable than you lose. You can track your performance over time and quickly identify when you are below your historical average and know you need to take a look at your trading strategy.

- You also want to set your maximum drawdown. Set a percentage, say 20 percent, of your account at the start of a trading cycle and decide that is your maximum drawdown. Ideally, as you progress in trading proficiency and take more consistent profits, you will want to limit your maximum draw down even more.

In the bigger picture, who controls the market? It's the old story, the bulls and bears, *"Big Money."* They are creating the market, making millions of trades every minute, every second, even milliseconds. On a side note, this is the very reason why day trading is an attractive option to many traders. But the market makers are large hedge funds, either one or multiple funds with the same idea. Either way, tracking their activity can be simple. That is not to say trading is easy, but large traders will, for the most part, take long term positions. It could take weeks, possibly months, to accumulate these positions, which allows us to track that trend in the market. Fortunately, there are charts (primarily candlestick charts) available to us that create a clear picture and signify entry points to trade. This is the subject of our next chapter.

CHAPTER 2

SWING TRADING STRATEGIES

CANDLESTICK CHARTS

I have mentioned *candlestick charts* as a valuable tool, so now let's take a closer look at what exactly they are. Primarily, it is a method of reading a price chart. The key components are the opening price, hi/lo, and closing price. Although, these components do depend on what time frame you're looking at (for example, an hourly chart may not have a closing price).

A candlestick chart tells us if big money is supporting higher prices, or dumping shares on the market creating lower prices. This chart is a genius in its simplicity, yet powerful if you have the discipline to takes its reading as absolute.

A candlestick chart shows us the relationship between the high/low, open and close in a specified time frame. The concept of supporting technical analysis is that *price discounts news*. If, as I advise, you take a dispassionate, logic-based approach to your trading, then you have to accept this concept: all factors determining price have already been 'baked' into the current price.

In the previous chapter, I explained how big money, mostly in the form of large funds, control the market. These funds have highly educated, very experienced research teams analyzing the numbers behind their investment decisions. We just need to discover where they are making the market and follow their lead.

This is technical analysis; we are relying on charts, not 'gut' feelings. Furthermore, swing traders are not investors in the traditional sense. We are not looking for a long-term hold position. We are looking for a catalyst and a spot to manage risk. Chart reading can help us earn a constant, reliable annual return. It is news and announcements that other investors are reacting to that provide us the peaks and valleys for swing trades. Looking at a chart, it is not hard to determine if prices are trending up, down, or sideways. This is where the *rules and guidelines* you have established come into play. Using those criteria, you define your edge within the charts.

It cannot be stressed enough, the swing traders who take the time to create a charting plan will possess a powerful scenario building machine. Technical analysis becomes a valid method only when you have structure. When you have an organized method of interpreting what the big money players are doing, then you will develop an edge against the market you can exploit.

So, to reiterate, one of the most common methods of analysis are *candlestick charts*. And the other is *moving averages*. You use these two metrics together, one to define a trend, and the other to define an entry signal. This allows you to interpret when big money is supporting a stock with new highs and higher lows, and the second allows you to manage risk (more on that later).

Chart reading gives us ideas and helps us locate profit targets, risk points, and probabilities. The real opportunity for swing traders is learning how to adjust positions and set expectations for share size, trade duration, and how many positions are correct for a particular market. This is where your growing expertise in technical analysis comes together with trade management skills. Those trade management skills you will have developed from taking the time setting rules and laying out your fundamentals.

READING A CANDLESTICK

A candlestick represents the complete price action for a given time — an hour, a day, a week, etc. To draw a candlestick, we simply draw a dash across the lowest opening price and dash across the highest closing price. Then, we would put a dot above the closing dash at the highest point the stock (for this example we'll call it a stock) reached in the trading period being charted. Then we would put a dot at the lowest point the stock reached in the trading period. By drawing two parallel lines connecting the dashes at the high and low closing points, we create the body of the candle. Then by drawing two lines from the top and bottom of the candle body to the dots representing the highest and lowest points, the stock reached we create the *wick* (sometimes, referred to as the *shadow*) of the candle. The candles of a candlestick chart are usually two colors, most often, green and red (or white and black if color charts aren't available).

If the green (or white) bullish close is *higher* than open, bearish red (or black), is the opposite. When the wick projects above a bullish close, you know buyers rejected a higher price within the session. If there is a very long wick, you know there was a significant correction within the trading session, even if the stock closes on a high, so there was immense selling pressure as traders took profits. If the wick is longer than the body, then there was extreme price rejection. If there is a wick extending below the bar of a body that closed high, that shows strength; there was no buy resistance.

A candlestick chart shows you who is in control, buyers or sellers. Color can be misleading when reading a candlestick chart. When we look at it (most charts are in color these days) and we see a lot of red and a lot of green. However, it's important to remember, what's important is the shape of the candlestick. You have to learn to look at the bodies of the candles, their position on the chart, their relation to the previous candle, and their position in relation to the price trend.

How not to trade candlestick patterns: Many new traders make this mistake, they see a long pattern of green candles and go long, then hit a market reversal, or make the same miscalculation for red candles in reverse. You don't want to trade candlestick patterns in isolation. Do not trade them in this manner.

BULLS VS. BEARS

Going back to who is in control of the market, with the candlestick, we see a time of play in a trading session, we can see the back and forth of the bulls and bears, and who's *'winning.'*

BULLS IN CHARGE   BEARS IN CONTROL   INDECISION

When reading a chart, a long green body with short wicks, we know the bulls were in charge. A red candle of the same pattern shows us the bears were in charge. Sometimes, though, we encounter a small body candle with more wick than the body (equal size, above and below). That tells you there was a great deal of **indecisiveness** in the market.

Or sometimes, we encounter a small body candle with a long wick below. That shows us the bears had control of the market, but the bulls rallied in the end. Alternatively, that same pattern, but with the long wick above shows the opposite, bulls had control, but the bears ultimately set the market.

A small body candle, but with long equal size wicks above and below, shows not only a great deal of indecisiveness but also a lot of market volatility, with no gains. It is important to know not only who was in control of the market at the close, but also who was in control during the trading session. Most short-term traders make the mistake of reading the net change from the previous close. This is wrong for most trades because you want to know the buying or selling pressure in your *current* trading session, you want to know the change from the *open*.

BASIC CANDLESTICK PATTERNS

There are a large number of patterns, but starting out, you just need to understand a few basic ones. You'll find most patterns are derivatives of these. However, to use candlestick charts, you need to know these patterns to see the market.

I will name them, but please keep in mind that remembering the names of the patterns is unimportant. The main thing is to learn to identify *the meaning* behind patterns.

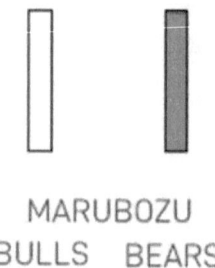

MARUBOZU
BULLS   BEARS

Marubozu, for example, is the name given to a specific candle type. One with no wicks (above or below). This shows the bulls (in a green body candle) dominated the entire trading session, so there was no price pushback, and as a result, no wick. A red *Marubozu* is, of course, the opposite with the bears controlling the entire trading session.

With that said, what does a *Marubozu* mean within the entire trading pattern? Price is always moving, so we have to look at price action. A bullish Marubozu can mean the continuation of an existing bullish trend, or the reversal of a downtrend trend. Similarly, a bearish Marubozu signifies that a bearish trend may intensify further, or that an uptrend may reverse. Marubozu is known as stand-alone patterns, in that they send a strong signal without any additional price confirmation.

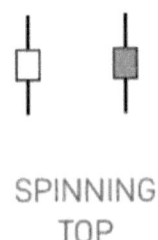

SPINNING TOP

Then there are **spinning tops**. These are the small bodied candles, with equal long wicks on top and bottom, I mentioned earlier, that represents huge market indecision. If we see a *spinning top* after a long advance, that demonstrates weakness in the bullish side of the market, and possibly the reversal of the trend. The converse is true for a bear market if we see a spinning top at the end of a long decline.

DOJI

A **Doji** is another pattern that you need to watch, actually one of the most common patterns. This is a candlestick with no candlestick body. It shows very little to no movement between open and close. The wicks of the *Doji* will show a tug of war between sellers and buyers, but ultimately close at/near the opening price. Usually, this is a sign of low volume trading, and like the *spinning top* this pattern shows indecision, but with no control gained by bulls or bears.

In addition, this pattern could be a sign that a *turning point* is developing. For example, the nearing of the uptrend to an end and the possible diminishing of the buying pressure can be signaled by a Doji after a green and long candlestick, or an advance.

When dealing with *Doji*, it should be remembered that a simple lack of buyers can decrease the price of the stock. Also, in order to maintain an uptrend, it is required to have a continued buying pressure. With that, a Doji may be more important after an uptrend and its appearance after a long green candlestick. Look for a bearish (red) candlestick after seeing a Doji in this placement to confirm the end of upwards buying pressure.

DRAGONFLY DOJI   GRAVESTONE DOJI

There are also different types of Doji patterns, depending on the length of the wick, and whether it favors a bullish or bearish trend. There are the *Dragonfly* and *Gravestone Dojis*.

- A *Dragonfly* forms when the close, high, and open are the same but a deep low makes a long wick, forming the Doji into an extended 'T' shape. This indicates that the trading is being dominated by the sellers, and during the session, the prices are driven lower, but buyers return late in the session and drove prices back to its opening price.
- The reversal of this (*Gravestone*), is of course, that there was strong early buy pressure, but sellers still loom to drive the price back to its low opening, reversing the T pattern. This shows price *resistance*, and possibly a bearish reversal.

More Complex Patterns

There are *thirty-two candlestick* patterns we could discuss in this book. However, realistically, there are only sixteen you should know, as most are derivatives of other patterns (i.e. for every bull, there is a bear) and the previous examples are quite common. Knowing instantly what they mean can be the difference between a losing and a winning trade.

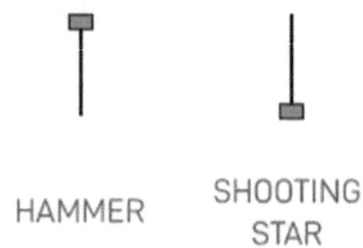

HAMMER   SHOOTING STAR

Let's start with the **Hammer** and **Shooting Star**. These patterns are similar to a *Dragonfly* and *Gravestone*, except for the fact that they have a small body, showing some movement between opening or close instead of almost the same place as with the Dojis.

- The *Shooting Star* is the bullish version of this pattern. It shows a bullish rejection, with sellers initially control, pushing the price low, creating the long bottom wick. Then with buyers coming in late and rejecting low prices.
- The *Hammer* is the bearish version of this pattern. Early buyers drove the price higher, but late sellers drove the price down below opening.

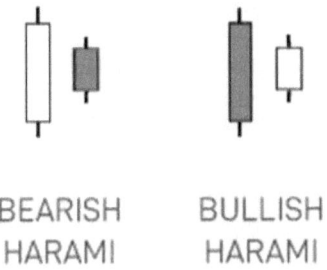

BEARISH HARAMI   BULLISH HARAMI

The **Harami**, which means *'pregnant'* in Japanese, is a two-session candlestick pattern. It is not concerned with reds and greens, but with the position. A *Harami* has a candle body that is smaller to the previous candle body. The wicks do not have to be contained within the body of the previous candle, although it is preferable if they are. The value of a *Harami*, whether it is high or low to the preceding candle body, is that it has the opposite color to that candle body (red or green, just so long as they are opposite).

The reason this (quite common) pattern is so important to recognize and to understand what it means, is that this pattern implies the price is about to turn. It's a warning pattern, a reversal pattern (although it may not indicate a really strong reversal). Often with Harami patterns, we see several days of tight range trading; this is sometimes referred to as *congestion*.

The Harami is just one example of *two position* patterns. Just as the *Marubozu, Doji, Spinning Top, Hammer/Shooting Star*, and *Dragonfly/Gravestone* are examples of the variety of *single position* patterns, two position patterns include (besides Harami) *Bullish Engulfing / Bearish Engulfing* and *Bullish Tweezers / Bearish Tweezers*.

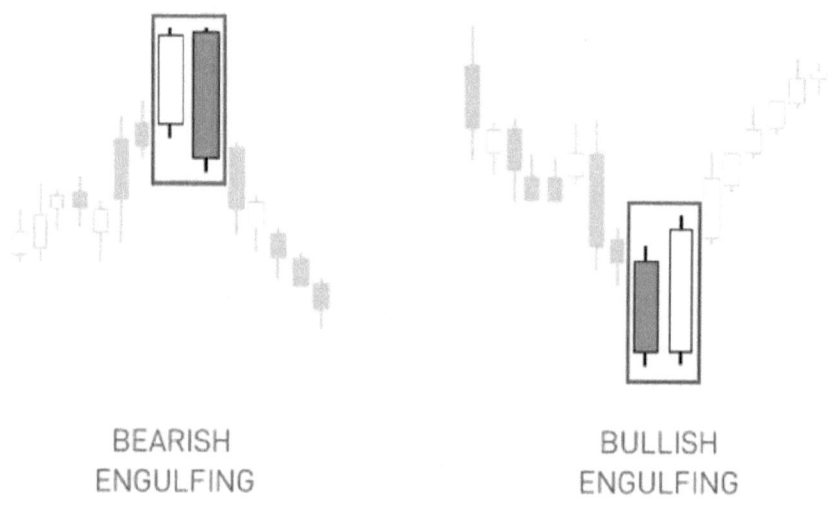

BEARISH ENGULFING   BULLISH ENGULFING

An **Engulfing pattern** (similar to a *Harami*) in its bullish version will show a green candle with a body and wick taller than the low and high of the previous red candle. This shows buyers bought at the lowest low and drove the price above the price of the previous candle, so we see very strong buyers. The *Bear Engulfing* pattern is the reverse of the previous example. Both are indicators of a possible trend reversal.

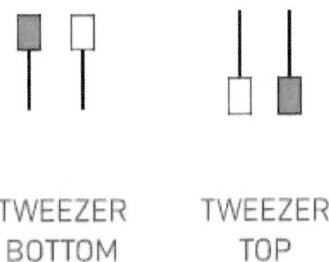

TWEEZER BOTTOM   TWEEZER TOP

Tweezer bottoms and tops show a reaction to lower prices. It, too, can be a powerful pattern, and also a very rare one. During a downward trend, a *Tweezer* pattern would have a small bodied red candle followed by a green candle of the same short body. Both candles will have long bottom wicks, which are again equal in size, and no upper wick, or very insignificant ones. The top variant of this pattern is its bearish reversal.

While it's important to understand the technical parameters of each of these patterns, you should not forget about the psychological dimension of trading. Let's take a look at the market movements behind this *Tweezer* pattern.

In psychological language, since the red candle in this pattern is small, it shows us some loss of momentum of the bearish trend, with the long downwards wick indicating the fear of the potential downside. Then comes the green candle, which indicates the bearish sentiment may be reversing. Yet, it also has a long bottom wick, indicating there is still some fear of further downward moves. But as the bottom of the wicks is equal, it also means the same level of support is holding. So we have a combination of indicators that the downward trend may reverse to bring an upward trend. This is a signal to you that you can go in for a long(er) position. You should always pay attention to those reversals patterns as they are triggers to enter the market.

BULLISH
MORNING STAR

BEARISH
EVENING STAR

Next, we get into *three position* candle patterns, such as *Morning/Evening Star*. The bullish *Morning Star* comprises of a long red candle that follows from the previous downtrend; this will be followed by a small bodied red candle (or a Doji), showing a significant gap in the chart where the candle body of the second one 'steps down.' The third candle body in this pattern is a green one, whose close is at least mid-point of the long red candle. This shows 1) sellers had control, 2) followed by indecision, 3) then buyers in control.

The bearish version of this pattern (*Evening Star*) is as you would expect the reverse, although it's worth stating that these patterns are rare, and even when they do appear, can be difficult to spot.

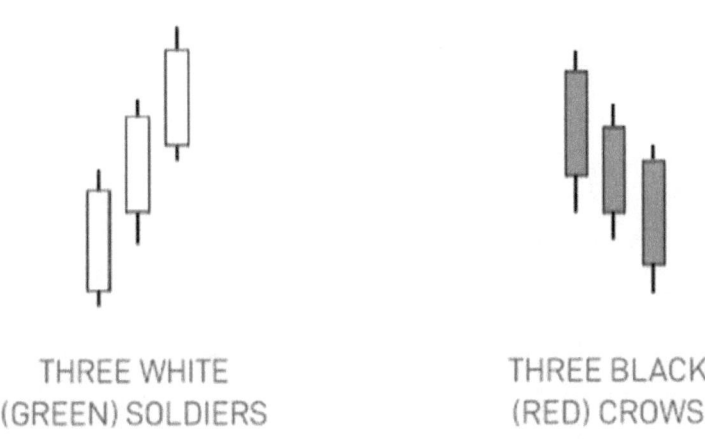

THREE WHITE (GREEN) SOLDIERS

THREE BLACK (RED) CROWS

Three White Soldiers (or green) is another reversal pattern that is bullish. Three green and long candles make this up while in a downtrend. Every one of these candles comes next to each other. They also open within the prior period's range and close near the high of the current period. The bears' complete route is also what this pattern is all about. The market is forced down to levels that are unrealistic because of these bears.

As a result, a massive 'offensive' is launched by the bulls. It has fed on its momentum for 3 consecutive sessions. This decimates any bears still left in the fray. To clarify, when I say *session*, I mean the candle, a complete session is not necessary to create this pattern. It can be created on an hourly chart as well as a daily chart.

As you should know by now, for every uptrend, there is a downtrend. **Three Black Crows** (or *red crows*) is the mirror bear version of *Three White Soldiers*.

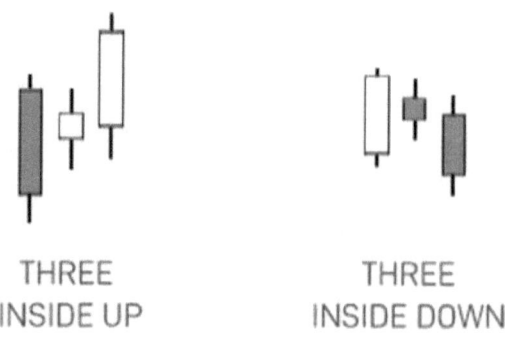

THREE INSIDE UP

THREE INSIDE DOWN

Next, we have **Three Inside Up** and **Three Inside Down**. This is another trio of three candles, but they can be difficult to spot. Although if you do spot this pattern, it is considered a fairly reliable one. *Three Inside Up* consists of a long red candle followed by two green candles that together exceed the movement of the previous red candle.

In this pattern, the bears have entrenched a downslide in prices, culminating in the tall red candle. But in the next session, the bulls have decided they've had enough of that and stand firm. In the following session, the bulls again resist downward price pressure and gain a small advantage.

Inside Down is, yes, the reverse of this pattern. And please note, like most *three candle patterns*, this is considered a reliable barometer of price reversal.

Now that you have (hopefully) a comprehensive understanding of candlestick charts and patterns, we can move onto the fun stuff. What these patterns mean to us in relation to the entry/exit points.

How to Trade Candlestick Patterns

So, how should you trade candlestick patterns? One way is to use trend area framework. Using the previous examples in candlestick patterns you should look for an entry trigger, this is also known as an *area of value* (a price range where at least 70% of trades have been executed during the previous trading sessions). You might surmise we would want to trade from an area of value, and as you learned in the previous chapter, candlestick patterns will help you define those areas. There are more indicators which are important to know, but to start with, let's formulate a trading strategy on an uptrend, and look for an entry trigger.

Remember, each candlestick chart is a reflection of the market sentiment, and with practice and experience, you can master the art of *trading by looking at the charts*. Since every trading story is told by the candles, you need to start asking yourself questions every time you see a trading chart. For instance, what is the trend that I'm seeing here? If the current market is running sideways, then what was the previous trend? Always look to see, are the highs getting higher or the lows lower? The candlestick bodies may suggest probabilities depending on the size of their bodies and their wicks.

When looking at candlestick bodies, don't forget the maxim: *a body in motion stays in motion*. There will always be some pull back on price, but when you discover a trend, in any direction, you know it will generally continue in that direction, so how to leverage that?

For this purpose we look for the price reversal patterns we discussed in the previous chapters. We can also analyze the chart as a whole. Obviously, any chart, whether it's an hour, a day, a week, or a month, will display swing lows and swing highs. When analyzing a time frame, do the swing highs close above the swing lows? A basic charting advice used by brokers and analysts to give them a snapshot of a trading period is to draw a line from every trading peak, then a parallel line from the bottom of every dip to determine if we are seeing a consistent uptrend.

As Swing traders, we don't care about the eases in the market. We want to enter at ease and anticipate the upthrust. And as we buy into the market at every ease of the upward trend, we move our stop losses up. Setting our stop losses at the candle above the previous price pullback. You don't know where the market peak is, but when the market eases, you'll be stopped-loss-out at least above your buy-in. You see the value in being diligent in moving stop loss orders up as the market advances, the closer you can set that order to the eventual market peak, the greater your profits.

Furthermore, you may not be finished with that stock, but as a swing trader, you keep buying back into the market. Instead of taking a long position, you have created the possibility of several profitable swings, if you are successful in finding an asset on an upward trend.

You do not always rely on stop-loss orders. There are sell swings, and you go into a trading cycle with a plan. As I noted previously, the volume will tell us if there is a potential positive trend for a given market. If the volume is declining, there is a strong indication of a downtrend. Remember, price only needs inactivity to decline, not sellers.

Moving Averages

Charts, as I have explained, are all about making sense of markets. Making sense of it in a visual way, to reveal patterns and suggest entry and exit points.

Another way to reduce confusion and noise in the markets and rationalizing them is *Moving Averages* (MA). These averages are commonly used in conjunction with candlestick charts.

While it can be a very useful tool in your trading tool belt, MA is a very simple thing, the average price over a given period. You can use 5, 10, 20, or 100, and sometimes, 200-day periods.

MA can smooth out the price action on the chart; it can let us see patterns we might otherwise miss. Especially overbought/oversold situations, which is a trading opportunity. Markets oscillate more around overbought/oversold situations.

A five-day time frame will still show a lot of oscillation, but a twenty-day period will smooth out random price actions to frame a trading period and can be quite useful. Going longer, to a 100 or 200-day periods, we'll probably see greater swings in activity, and might give us some perspective on where the market has been, but for swing purposes, it is not that useful.

On the candle chart, if the movement of the price is above the MA line (for this example, we'll say 20 days), then we can identify an uptrend. Conversely, if the movement of the price is below the MA line, then we can confirm a downtrend. The post where price breaks the MA line usually implies a trend reversal.

MA lines can also define areas of price support or resistance. We can watch to see if the price is moving towards the MA line, and does it break it or bounce back? Usually, if the price is in an uptrend, it will find support at the MA line, and if in a downtrend, there will be resistance at the MA line.

However, always remember, MA is an indication of past prices, and therefore, a *lagging indicator*. It is not a warning of price, but an indicator of a trend change.

As a trader, the MA will help you identify entry and exit points. If the MA is below the price trend line, it's acting as support and gives you a clear indication of where to place your stop loss, just underneath the MA line (since that would indicate the price has lost its support at that level.
If the price trend is above the MA line, it is acting as price resistance. When the movement of the price goes above the

MA line, you again have a strong indicator that resistance has been broken, and you should place a stop loss just above the MA line.

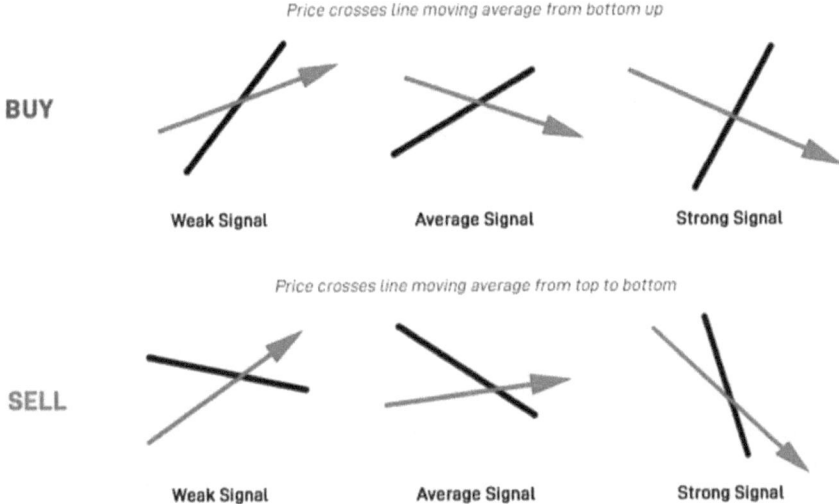

The interesting thing about MAs is that they can be used alone or in conjunction with other MAs. You can place two MA lines on a chart, reflecting two different time frames, e.g. a short-term and a longer-term trend, and you have the opportunity to trade using MA crossovers. For example: place ten days MA line and a twenty day MA line. When shorter period MA line crosses above a longer-term MA line, that could indicate an uptrend and a buy signal. And when a shorter period MA line crosses below a longer period MA line, it is considered bearish.

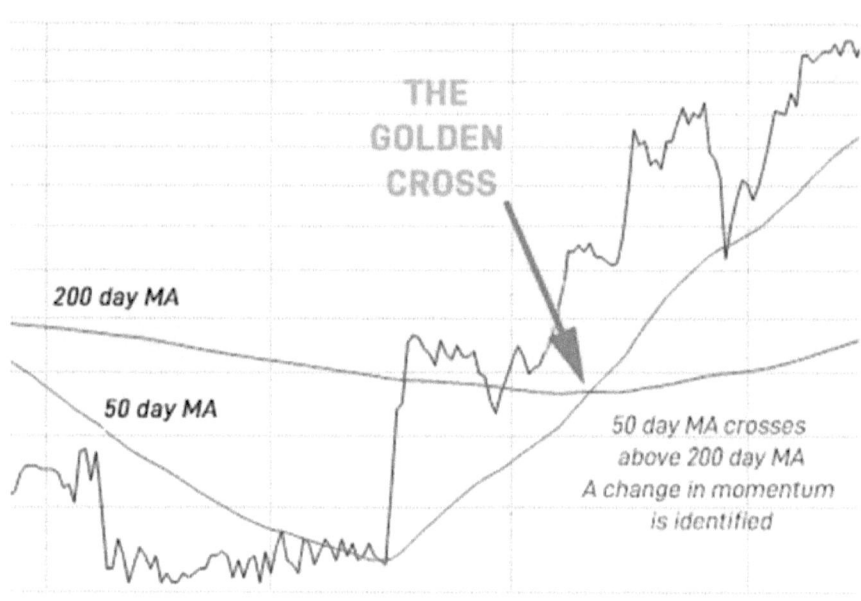

No matter which two periods you use, this principle will remain the same. Long position investors will usually use 50 to 200-day MA lines, but that is not going to be optimum for swing trading strategies. As a swing trader, you will likely be focused mainly on shorter-term trends.

There are three main types of MAs. So far, I have been referring to *Simple Moving Averages (SMA)* which is the closing price of a given period, divided by that period, so a five-day SMA would be the closing price divided by five. You could then plot the average price over those five days. Moving average derives its name from the average constantly moving forward in the advancing period, with the last day being dropped from the next five-day plot. In a

Simple Moving Average, all prices are given equal weight regarding averaging.

The downside of this is because the equal weight is given to each rating period, the SMA is slow to respond to a rapid price change. This is something that should concern us as swing traders. To counter this, we can use *weighted* or *exponential MAs (EMAs)*. Although calculated differently, they respond faster to price action, give more weight to recent trading periods, less weight to older periods and reflect a quicker shift in trading sentiment. I will not be giving details on EMAs in this book, but you may certainly find a lot of resources online to learn about this type of moving averages (for example, here: www.fidelity.com/learning-center/trading-investing/technical-analysis/technical-indicator-guide/ema).

BUILDING BLOCKS

So by combining candlestick charts and MAs and monitoring volume, we can combine tools and have an informed look at the market. However when developing a trading plan or your swing trading strategy, you also need to define in advance what your market entry point indicators will be. Don't mix and match your plan as needs arise.

Generally, the market has *four specific cycles*; there is no other movement a stock can make. The key to trading successfully is knowing where you are in this cycle, whether it's a one day chart or a one week chart. You have to establish what you're going to use. You can't adjust your charts to give you a *buy* reading. It will just give you a false reading, and that is a recipe for disaster.

The market cycle exists in any market trend, whether in an overall uptrend, downtrend or if the stock or asset is ranging in a sideways motion. There will be the market cycle within those trends. So, here are the cycles:

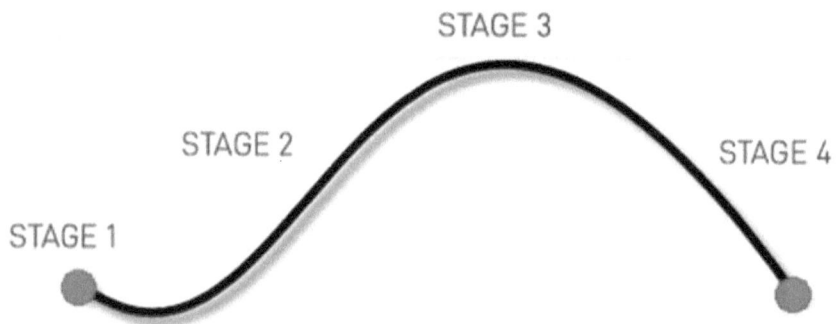

- *stage one* of the cycle is the price pullback or dip,
- *stage two* identifies an upward trend,
- *stage three* is a market peak,
- and *stage four* is a downward trend.

Once you're able to identify where you are in the cycle using the analytical methods outlined in this book, we can identify an entry point, which should be *stage two* in the cycle, where we want to *buy, buy, buy*.

The only way to win at trading is to correctly identify the buy area, i.e. stage two, and to sell at or near the price peak, or sell short on the downtrend. Losses in trading happen when traders do not take the time to correctly analyze the trading cycle, or they let greed motivate them and buy too close to the price peak. Then, they let fear motivate them and sell at the bottom of the cycle.

A good practice is to look at a chart from a sector you plan to trade in. We've been primarily talking about securities, but you could also use a commodity or currency, and try to identify cycles on a *one-day chart*. This will be more difficult than a weekly chart and certainly more so than a monthly chart, but the challenge will help hone your skills at analysis. This is what swing trading is, this is not applicable to other types of trading.

Again, it bears repeating; *stage two* is your critical buy point. This is where you make money. Stage three is the topping point and too late to enter; this is ideally where you want to be exiting the market having successfully captured the swing.

The downtrend is always the second part of the cycle. If you see a downtrend, back up to see the beginning of the cycle with the uptrend that allowed that asset to trend down. There are not many ways to lose in this example, and that's coming into the cycle *too late* and hanging on *too long*. Most buyers who have hung on too long into the downward cycle tend to leave all at once, and in turn, that creates the climatic part of the decline. Ironically, once these last batches of traders exit the market, the worst is over.

The market, whether it is a stock or commodity, can only be in one of the four stages at any given time. The successful market player has a collection of approaches for each stage. Although, ideally, you are buying in stage two, and selling into the bear market at stage four.

Now, this may seem like a simplistic strategy. However, the reality is the market in real time can be very difficult to read. While it is critically important to identify cycle stages, there are also *transition points* or *transition phases* that cloud which stage a stock is in. Transitional phases tend to be the most difficult periods or points of trade. They are choppy and very volatile. It is safe to say that the highest degree of market mastery is obtained when the trader can not only identify market stages but also handle *transitional phases*.

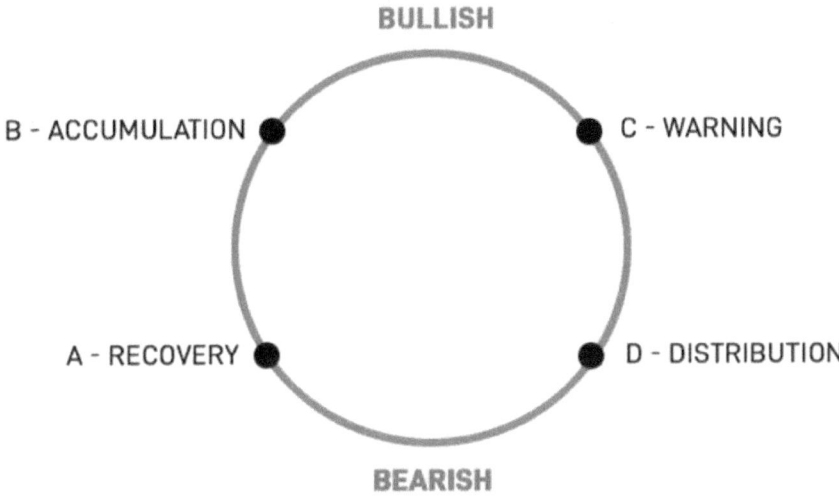

If the stages are 1, 2, 3, and 4, the transition phases can be called A, B, C, and D, but more specifically, we would call them *recovery, accumulation, warning,* and *distribution*. Accumulation (B) would be the transition phase between stage 2 and 3. And the *warning* (C) phase would be the transition between stage 3 and 4.

Some of the best times to get into a trade are the transitional phases. The reason for this is if we can anticipate a transition phase, then we will see the greatest price expansion, vs. if we wait for confirmation that we are really in a bullish market.

To do this, we must look for the transition, not just the market reversal signal.

So, how to recognize price breakouts? When we look at price action and get near previous highs and previous lows, that's generally where the market turns. Then, sometimes, we get price breakouts, but let us talk first about false breakouts since there are plenty of them, which is more common than an actual price breakout.

This isn't necessarily a bad thing; this scenario too can give us a low risk, potentially high reward trade situation. Let's take the hypothetical example of a market that breaks through a new low below the previous session's lowest price. We might expect to see a collapse of price support and a breakout low. But as noted, false breakouts are far more common than a real price breakout, since the bull/bear market cycle is much more the natural equilibrium of the market than sustained rallies (in short trading time frames). When we see a price decline below the previous low, we know the probability of a rally is more likely than continued sell-off. Ideally, we spot this sell-off and watch for some point of support, even a few candles of sideways movement should be enough of a confirmation. If we put a stop loss on the previous session's low close, we can confidently buy into the market without too much risk. And again, more often than not, a steep sell-off precedes a price reversal and upwards trend, and in some cases, a serious rally.

While honing trading skills is certainly advantageous, you can, with little practice, begin to swing trade successfully (but manage your risk carefully). The following are some buy and sell setups. The Key Buy set up is made up of only a few basic criteria, the Key is one to five bar trading gains on the upside, and a trader can often use this criterion to buy without another guide. In a Key Buy set up, the emphasis is on highs, not the close but highs in the trading session.

An important statistical fact to consider is that five consecutive battles cannot be won by bears and bulls consistently. Each side typically sees a reversal after three to five rallies. Also, and this is very important to pay attention to: if 5 or more battles can be won by bears and bulls in a row, a loss will be the price paid in the end for such an abnormal winning streak.

Previously in our analysis of candlestick charts and patterns and what they can do for you, I noted how powerful a three-session or three bar pattern was.

Also, I explained how emotion affects the majority of investors. So, if you see a three bar up pattern, you should be thinking *sell*, as that's a sure sign greed is dominating that market and emotional investors are jumping in, meaning they are late to the rally. Three, or better, four to five bars down, would be a strong buy signal.

With what are really simple trade practices, hopefully, by now, you are gaining a better understanding of these building blocks. Experience will hone these skills, but going in with these tools on your belt, you should be able to avoid confusion and profit-killing indecision. As you master these concepts, you will find that you will rarely be on the wrong side of a trade. The ultimate profits will always be a factor of the amount of capital put in. But, with a proper trading plan and patience, you can outperform the market long term.

Over sixty-five percent of all trading losses can be attributed to being on the wrong side of the market.

More Trading Patterns

Continuing with the goal of combining the tools we have put in place to analyze data and successfully trade, let's take a look at some other patterns that combine candlesticks and MA trend lines (which will be EMAs).

First, there is the *ascending uptrend pattern*, this is when a stock continues to show growth, but as it trends upwards, hits a peak, a sell-off, before hitting new price support and continuing its upward trend, peaking again above its previous peak. We can determine this trend with an EMA trend line. When we start to see the stock close consistently for several sessions below the EMA trend line, we know the stock is on its downswing.

This is a pattern that will develop over a thirty to hundred-day (or longer) time frame. Meaning, within it, there will be an opportunity for swing trades. When the stock begins to close above the EMA trend line at a point above the previous cycle's lowest closing, that will likely be the start of a buy signal. Using the candlestick patterns discussed in earlier chapters will help determine the bottom of the cycle, and find a price entry point. An ascending upswing pattern is a pattern that a trader could exploit for several upswings, and is sometimes, colloquially known as *'Catching a Wave.'*
Trading on a horizontal pattern is perhaps a more identifiable pattern, sometimes referred to as *'Stuck in a Box'* as the stock (for these examples, we'll refer to the asset in question as a stock) the stock moves in a sideways pattern. In this pattern, peaks and valleys close at roughly the same point. For example, say we see price resistance on stock at $29 and price support at $24 over several cycles. We can set the EMA line at $28, and again, likely capture several successful swings within this pattern. There is another

pattern strategy, this one more aggressive and a counter-trend trade. As the market moves in an uptrend, you will experience price resistance. However, you have to be careful as the price can reverse against you quite quickly.

This is somewhat similar to profiting from a false breakout that we discussed in an earlier chapter. But in this scenario, we are looking at an upswing market and a false breakout high. Sometimes known as, *'Fade the Move,'* unlike catching the wave of an uptrend, we look to selling short on the downswing, as investors who went long on what they thought was a breakout up trend find themselves trapped, and fuel selling as they abandon their position.

Chapter 3

Practical Tips and Tricks

Rules

Here are the rules you should always keep in mind in order to be a successful and profitable swing trader.

Always have a trading plan, yes I know I may sound like a broken record by now, but repetition never hurts when talking about a critical component of trading successfully. You should never begin trading on a whim. If you have gained nothing else from this book (which I sincerely hope is not the case), know that you *cannot enter swing trading without a set of guidelines in place*. You must know your entry levels, your stop loss levels, and what your initial trading plan is. Even if your strategy is unsuccessful, you will have a record of what didn't work and go forward from there. As I have said (also repeatedly), trading on emotion is a recipe for disaster. Please, take the time to prepare yourself and give yourself a roadmap. Remember, trading is a business, so treat it that way. Calculate the risk for every dollar traded.

Remember the fundamentals when formulating a trading strategy, generally, trade with the trend, but as a swing trader, you want to fade the short term trend against the long-term trend. Almost invariably before the market goes up, it goes down first. You want to put your entries where the masses put their stops. Most people put their stops at very predictable places; you do not want to be following the masses. Another fundamental to remember is, a good trade is award trade. Meaning, if you have done your research, you are more likely to make a good trade.

Also, **invest in your tools**. In the era of online trading, the market can move very fast; you will need a fast, reliable Internet connection to ensure you are not cut off from trading at critical junctures. Yes, stop-loss orders do a great deal to manage risk without monitoring your trade minute by minute. But while executing a trade, do you want to find yourself in the position of being suddenly unable to connect with your account? I didn't think so. Furthermore, a reliable Internet connection should mean *Ethernet* and *not WiFi*. Yes,

Ben Hockett famously traded $79 million in *Credit Default Options* from a pub in England using their WiFi connection, but even then, a big part of the story was that the pub's WiFi stayed reliable over the four days of online transactions - so use Ethernet.

As well, ***invest in a reliable computer and good software*** (please, no free Internet downloads). Money upfront on good hardware and software will save you money down the line. In addition to a good, reliable computer, you should also have at least one portable hard drive to back up data with. They can be bought for a little as a $100, and save you a great deal of frustration and agony if your computer ever goes down.

Speaking of safety and backups, a ***stop loss order*** is a must. Never enter an order without entering an arresting stop loss order at the same time. While it is certainly possible to enter stop-loss orders later, why take the unnecessary risk. Novice and experienced traders alike fail to put in place stop-loss orders after placing a trade as they get caught up in capturing the swing and maximizing profits. When money is on the line, people are amazing at talking themselves out of prudent measures. So, place the stop-loss order when you place the order and save yourself from potentially catastrophic losses (true, that's worst case scenario, but why expose yourself to it in the first place?).

The above should go hand-in-hand with **_knowing your exit in advance_**. If you are following the strategies outlined in this book, then you know the critical component of these strategies is knowing your exit. Otherwise, you are simply playing on a whim, something (in case I haven't made abundantly clear by now) you should always avoid.

When you embark on swing trading, whether it is a part-time venture to make extra money, or as a path to a career change, **_always trade with risk capital only_** to avoid emotional trading and remain analytical in your approach. The best way to do that is trading with the money that is okay for you to lose. If it is only $500, better to start with that amount and trade using practiced technical strategies, rather than start trading in desperation as you try to recoup losses you couldn't afford, thereby, worsening the situation (it can happen faster than you think). The flip side of that is emotional traders who plan their strategies can and do make consistent profits with only small amounts of capital.

Similar to the above rule is knowing **_when to take a break_**. Many traders, again, both experienced and novice lose money when they do not see the signs of burnout. Swing trading can be a very engrossing activity, even when done part-time. Reading charts, analyzing data, and looking for profitable swings requires a significant intellectual investment, and it can take a higher toll on you than you might realize. Burnout is probably the single biggest contributor to trading losses outside of a market crash, and is far, far more common. Don't be afraid to take time off. Try to see the big picture; you're trading to make money to make your life better, don't let trading define your life. And as noted, spending too much time and energy on trading will only lead to cloudy judgment and losses. Far better to take a week off, reassess the market and your positions, and begin again refreshed and reenergized.

Never stop learning. As you might have realized in reading this book, there is a great deal of information to digest to be a successful trader. You do not have to know every detail and minutia of candlesticks, moving averages, and the mountain of information that could be compiled around technical data. You need to know the concepts that I have outlined in this book and build experience. But, that doesn't mean you should never stop learning. While the amount of data and its various interpretations and applications can seem daunting, it is a process. Learning how to evaluate data better is something you will continue to learn, as long as you remain open to it. As well, technology changes too, and you have to be aware of those changes and how they may affect your trading.

One thing experience will teach you is that ***once you get it, you never forget it***. Like riding a bike, or perhaps like learning to snorkel, motions that seemed hard to coordinate suddenly come together and you never forget how to do them. The same can be said for trading, combining data points to create a profitable trading strategy might be cumbersome and difficult at first, but there will come that moment when it will click.

Another rule or principle you will discover as you gain experience in swing trading is that while anyone can learn it, only about twenty percent follow the rules (in an echo of the Pareto principle outlined at the beginning of this volume). Why do only twenty percent develop strategies and follow their own rules to a successful trading career? Most fall prey to common pitfalls before they can become profitable traders. How to avoid these errors and ensure you will stay long enough to develop the skills and mindset to become a profitable trader? I hope by now you realize that the answer to this is all about sticking to the rules, learning to improve them where needed and developing your experience.

So, *document, verify and identify your strategy and results*. They will give you a paper trail; it's like how your game films give you something to look back on and learn from success and mistakes, part of building a foundation strategy. Number a repeatable pattern and measure its profitability. Generally, the simpler and more straightforward your rules, the more robust and evergreen your strategy will be. For example, trend following, that's the basis of price movement. This does not mean it is always profitable but start with it as a basic principle. This can help you minimize losses. As you gain experience, certain strategies can become more nuanced, but a baseline strategy has to start somewhere.

Put the odds in your favor and trade with the trend. One of the biggest mistakes traders make is that for one reason or another, they cannot trade with the trend they have decided so that it would seem that they know the real top of the market or the real bottom. For example, if in 2017 you traded against cryptocurrencies, you would have traded yourself out of substantial profits. If a market is on a substantial uptrend for six months or a long downtrend, why do some traders, based on their 'gut' feelings, insist they can pinpoint the exact top or exact bottom of a market? That is a mystery, but not a habit you should follow. There are very experienced traders who have convinced themselves of this notion, and some have cost themselves small fortunes in trying to be a contrarian trader.

Another mistake, and this one is far more common, is **setting stop losses far too tight**. Yes, risk management is important, but you have to give the trade a chance to move in your favor.

Also, always remember to **look for stocks or assets trading at higher than usual relative value**, and that is how you should set your watch lists since high volume is where you will find entry point indicators. Small caps that fall into this category will be difficult to find. There are plenty of investment gurus out there who will try to sell you on small caps and penny stocks and their *'tremendous upside potential'*. But these stocks are heavily promoted and controlled by venture capitalists who often manipulate the stock in their favor. Small caps may look enticing because of the potential to go from $0.10 to a $1.00 seems like it should be possible. But penny stocks can languish in the basement for years with little trading activity. Plus, there is little transparency on these stocks, and that is, by design, as promoters are often hiding the real value of these stocks.

So remember - large cap is where you will find the consistent volume, and this is where you should be scanning for entry points.

Commodities are something we haven't touched on a great deal in this volume, but all of the trading principles outlined here are certainly just as applicable to commodity trades as they are to stocks. In fact, just like large-cap stocks, commodities offer high trading volume and transparency; they can and do make excellent vehicles for swing trades. We have also not gone into specifics on currency trading, which, like commodities, also offer ample opportunities for swing trades. The reason for this is not an omission, but simply to keep this volume more focused on the basics of swing trading overall, rather than delve into specialties that could be entire volumes of their own to cover comprehensively.

BACKTEST

To have the trading strategy tested on related historical data, the process of *backtesting* is conducted. This is to make sure that it is viable before a trader takes a risk on an actual capital. A strategy's trading can be simulated by a trader over a right period. The results can also be analyzed by them for the levels of risk and probability.

To try and simplify that a bit, at a high level, the goal is to validate your strategy across as much in the sample and out of sample data that you can get your hands on. Basically, go back over as many charts as you have access to and look at your trading rules, and the results namely, did you make money? And don't forget to account for commission costs.

Ultimately, you're looking to validate the robustness of your rules, making adjustments where necessary, but very importantly, you do not want to excessively adjust rules and parameters, as you will run the risk of curve fitting your strategy to your data set.

One way of backtesting is to *paper trade*. That is to set up a practice account and test your trading rules and strategies. The problem with paper trading is you have no emotional connection to the trades; you're not risking anything. It can be a worthwhile exercise in the short term to get comfortable with the process of swing trading, and becoming comfortable with the mechanics of it so you can enact trades swiftly and efficiently. However eventually you will have to risk your capital. Taking this step is better done sooner rather than later. You can become too comfortable with paper trading, feeling that you are developing your trading skills, but decisions you make in paper trading will inherently be different from those you make when trading real money, and therefore, paper trading very quickly loses its utility.

The good news though is that you do not have to risk a great deal of capital to begin swing trading. Through the course of this book, I have always advocated a *go slow, risk management* approach.

By the time you have finished your backtest process, you should have a pretty good idea that your strategies are working, and that you have solid risk management rules and place (and that you pay attention to them). What benchmarks you should be looking for in a backtest is your *winning percentage, risk profile,* how many *losses in a row* you can sustain, and what your *drawdown* is, and *how long you can sustain it*. That is what you are looking for, so going forward; you can feel confident at trading at the risk level you've set.

If you don't find your backtest produces less than favorable results, you're going to have to rethink your strategy, as tweaking a data sets that aren't producing the results you want is more likely to make matters worse than produce any radical change. You might be paying close enough attention to spreads, which is a common mistake for novice swing traders. However, whatever the problem, it is advisable to start over with a new strategy at that point. Even when you start trading successfully, you can't sit back and watch the profits roll in. You'll need to constantly monitor your system and verify everything is operating as your backtest and live trading experience suggest.

Sooner or later, you will experience a larger drawdown that you are used to. Sometimes, despite using sound technical analysis, there will be erratic downtrends in the market. Fortunately, they are rare, but you will eventually encounter this scenario. In this situation, reassess your inputs. The problem may be an unexpectedly low price breakout. However, if you are consistently losing or making smaller than expected gains on an uptrend, which should be a favorable trading situation, then something may be off on your analysis, and you need to reassess again. Your data might be giving you misleading turning points in the market cycle. Coming in too late on a trend, even by one or two trading sessions, can mean the difference between a profitable trade and a loss, and it may also create a cascade effect. Whereby, you try to recapture a profitable position, but your trading cycle is pushing you further and further out of favorable position, buying too late, selling too far into the downtrend. Usually, this is a situation where a bad data read is compounded by emotional trading as you double down on your losses.

If you're following a bad position in the hope you can turn it around, don't. Stop, take the loss, and reassess before you turn a bad loss into a catastrophic loss. Even the most profitable trading strategy in the world can turn disastrous in the hands of an overly aggressive trade. Of course, the best way to avoid these situations in the first place is to backtest data regularly.

COSTS OF TRADING

Starting out a fundamental question is *which trading platform broker you should use*? The reality is - there is no one specific broker who is best, they are all different and offer different options.

Initially, many novice swing traders choose a broker based on fees. The reason for this is to reduce costs, especially if you are starting out with a small account and have little in the way of risk capital. Obviously, there is a trade-off in options when dealing with a low fee brokerage.

Overall, the costs of trading are trending lower, and you have a growing list of low-cost options. With as little as $500, you can start with a **Robinhood** account and use their investing app (not an endorsement). They don't charge commissions, which is obviously a plus. Although if you're starting out with $500 of risk capital, don't expect to quit your day job. Still, $100 of annual return on $500 is actually pretty good.

Just the same if you are using limited risk capital, then trading costs are a substantial factor. If you make twenty trades per month (that's forty transactions, don't forget) and you are paying $10 commission per trade, that's $400 per month, so clearly, you need to consider your broker before you start trading. No matter what your break-even point is, brokerage costs can quickly eat into any potential profits.

Then, as I noted, you also have to consider what services are provided, or not provided. What services you can't do without and what you don't need.

Robinhood is a free trading platform, though mobile only, and very limited in research tools and technical analysis. So if you are trying to apply the tools learned in this book and those gained and perfected through continued experience, this will not be the best fit, despite the attraction of no trading fees.

Lightspeed (again not an endorsement) is a newer online broker, offering trades at as little as $2 commission per trade. They are primarily set up for day traders though but certainly offer much more in research tools and technical analysis than Robinhood.

Scottrade (not an endorsement) is where many novice traders start out, including swing traders. They are very user-friendly and cater to new and beginner traders. They offer research tools that are easy to use and offer a mobile app as well (although that utility is of negligible value to swing traders). However, their commission rates start at $7 per trade, and that can up fast, but on the other hand, may force you into more disciplined trading.

Interactive Brokers (not an endorsement), is not as retail friendly as Scottrade, but it does have a more attractive commission structure. It also offers more to tech-savvy users, and if you wish to hone your technical analysis skills, (which you should) their platform, while a little more challenging in the beginning, could pay off later.

What online tools do you need to successfully trade (if you don't want to pay a premium to online brokers)? Three websites you should bookmark to find good trading vehicles and research tools are as follows (and again, none of these is an endorsement for any product or service):

- *__Finviz.com__* is a free service (with paid upgrades) that bills itself as the ultimate stock portal. While I can't vouch for it being the 'ultimate' anything, it can certainly be a valuable tool in researching stocks. It is very user-friendly, especially for novice traders, with many filters available to narrow down performance metrics and tailor them to your trading criteria.

- *__Stockcharts.com__* is also free (and also has upgrades available, with many more options that come with the premium product). It is perhaps not as easy to use as Finviz, but it does offer a lot of data across a large variety of markets and is much more customizable.

- *__TC2000__*, again this is a free and pay product, but most features require a paid subscription. It is, by far, the most advanced of all three. With it, you can write code and truly customize the platform to your needs. Most users use their paid version to unlock all options, and the cost is about $30-40. It is a steeper learning curve for novice investors to use.

- Finally, I would also mention *__ThinkOrSwim__* (once again, not an endorsement). This has become increasingly popular trading software offered by Ameritrade. It provides user-friendly research tools and a customizable scanner to help you find market entry points. It is also very user-friendly and geared towards beginner and self-directed traders, although, it is also geared towards holders of Ameritrade accounts. Still, it can be a useful tool to have even if you aren't trading through Ameritrade.

Goals

Most trading is boiled down to two types, *wealth trading* and *trading* for *income*. Swing traders are usually all about *income* trading. But for reference, we can look at wealth building style, or core trading, which is over weeks, and more often months, for longer-term accounts that are not time sensitive.

It can be important though to look at wealth building style, for perspective on the long-term market. To trade the market successfully, remember you're competing against experienced traders, so build up your own experience slowly. If you treat trading as a journey, that is a better mindset than trying to make money fast.

Obviously, everyone wants to make money. However, risking just one percent of your capital per trade will help you build experience and learn without dissipating your capital. Realize that you may have more losses than winners.

In swing trading, you have to be thinking 100 trades ahead, and how to capitalize over the average on those 100 trades. To meet your swing trading goals, you need a strategy and the discipline to follow it. To be consistent, you need to know when to adapt.

That might sound like a contradiction, but it's not. Adapting doesn't mean you must *change* your trading plan. Adapting means you need to understand when to step on the gas and when to slow down. It means learning when to be in cash and when to add aggressively to winning positions. Inexperienced swing traders often believe that following a strategy is a *black and white* process. When I say adapt, I don't mean change your strategy. It is implying that you should adjust how you apply it.

One giant psychological hurdle to overcome is believing every trade is the same. It's simply not true. Some trades have a higher probability and should be managed differently. To succeed, you need to know what these scenarios look like, so you are ready to make quality decisions. You need to prepare yourself with a decision making process before it happens. It's also important not to get caught up in comparing yourself to experienced/professional traders on Wall Street who claim to be making extraordinary profits on a consistent basis. When you're just starting out, the entire process should really be more of a competition *with yourself* – a focus on steady personal growth.

CONCLUSION

Hopefully, in reading and studying this book, you have realized that while not easy, swing trading is accessible and potentially profitable to anyone. What I also hope you have taken away from this book is to trade intelligently. There is a difference between trading intelligently and conservatively. It is possible to lose money trading conservatively; it will just take longer. Managing risk is crucial to successful swing trading, but that does not mean you shouldn't take advantage of a clear trade signal to its fullest advantage when presented with one.

The key is technical analysis or technical fundamentals. Starting slow and building experience and proficiency in your research and analytical skills will give you the confidence to risk more capital on your trades. Not because you are emotionally-driven, but because you have learned through research and practice what clear buy and sell signals are.

To get to this point, as I have noted, start by trading *no more than one percent of your capital* and concentrate on averaging *more wins than losses,* and to *minimize your losses* with the prudent risk management techniques we have discussed. This is the path to leveraging a small amount of capital to large gains. It won't happen overnight or even in a month. But throughout a year, you can see substantial gains relative to low risk and minimal capital.

Do you want to make trading a career? If you do, swing trading is an excellent training school. You have read how many techniques there are to master, yet that is still no barrier to entry. I hope that you have enjoyed this book and that it has encouraged you to go forward with your trading goals and profit from the building blocks of knowledge laid out here. Trading, besides the profit reward, can be an enjoyable career, whether done part-time or as your primary source of income. Its intellectual challenges will benefit you in ways beyond the acquisition of wealth.

I sincerely hope that this volume will be the first brick in the groundwork of your trading foundation and the beginning of a rewarding of not just profits and earnings, but knowledge as well.

Best of luck,
Kenneth

APPENDIX

Glossary of Swing Trading Terms

Area of value – in trading, a measure where heavy trading volume occurs (~2/3 of trades). Area of value is used to determine potential areas of support and resistance.

Backtesting – the process of testing a trading strategy on actual historical data.

Bull/bear market – presence of "bulls" indicates rising prices of shares and other securities, presence of "bears" means decreasing prices of securities.

Congestion – several days of tight range trading, e.g. where the demand of holders, willing to exit is matched with the supply of new traders.

Commodity – a basic good used in commerce that is interchangeable with other *commodities* of the same type (i.e. with no regard to who produced them). Examples of commodities are raw materials, agricultural, mining products - iron ore, copper, sugar, coffee, rice, wheat etc.

Day trading – a trading strategy where a tradable asset is held for a short duration of time (max a period of a single day's trading) with the intention of profiting from small price fluctuations.

Dead market – a market with no movement up or down (i.e. no swing to capitalize on).

Doji – a candle type in a candlestick chart with no candlestick body. Doji shows very little to no movement between open and close.

Engulfing pattern – a two-session candlestick pattern, where the second candle body 'engulfs' the first candle body. Typically, considered to be a trend reversal pattern.

Fibonacci arcs – typically, drawn as half-circles based on Fibonacci levels, applied to the distance between two swing points on a chart (high and low).

Fibonacci retracement – defined by taking the extremum points on a stock chart and dividing the distance between the points by Fibonacci ratios (23.6%, 38.2%, 61.8%, 78.6%). After the levels are identified, horizontal lines are used to locate potential support and resistance levels.

FINRA (Financial Industry Regulatory Authority) – in the United States, a non-profit self-regulatory organization authorized by the U.S. Congress to protect investors by making sure the broker-dealer industry operates fairly and honestly.

FOREX (FOReign EXchange) – the market in which currencies are traded (i.e. one currency is converted into another). The largest and most liquid market in the world.

Harami – a two-session candlestick pattern, where the second candle body is smaller to the previous candle body. Typically, considered to be a trend reversal pattern.

Hammer/Shooting star – a candle type in a candlestick chart with a very small candlestick body, showing some movement between opening or close instead of almost the same place as with the Dojis. *Hammer* – the bearish version of the pattern, *Shooting star* – bullish version of the pattern.

Higher highs/lows – a series of high and low price points in a price uptrend.

Intraday – 'within the day', price movements of a given security over the course of one trading day.

Large-cap stocks – the most approachable and the most transparent to investors, typically refers to companies with $10 bln + market capitalization (hence, "large cap").

Lower lows/highs – a series of low and high price points in a price downtrend.

Market cycle – the trajectory of movement between the two latest highs / lows, consists out of 4 stages: price pullback, upward trend, market peak, downward trend.

Marubozu – a candle type in a candlestick chart, with no wicks above or below, shows the bulls (in a green body candle) dominated the entire trading session. A red *Marubozu* is the opposite with the bears controlling the entire trading session.

Moving average – average stock price over a given period.

Paper trading – a simulated trading without any risk of losing your money.

Pareto Principle (*aka 80/20 rule*) – 80% of the effects come from 20% of the causes.

Resistance level – a price level where an uptrend is expected to pause due to a decrease in demand (i.e. a sell-off point).

Retracement – a short-term price correction during an overall larger upward or downward trend.

Simple Moving Averages (*SMA*) – arithmetic moving average, calculated by adding recent closing prices, divided by the number of time periods in the calculation average.

Spinning top – a candle type in a candlestick chart – a small bodied candle, with equal long wicks on top and bottom, represents major market indecision.

Stop-loss order – an order where the broker is instructed to sell the stock when its price reaches a particular low level.

Support level - a price level where a downtrend is expected to pause due to an increase in demand.

Swing trading – a trading strategy where a tradable asset is held between one day to several weeks in an effort to profit from price changes (otherwise known as 'swings').

Tweezer - a two-session candlestick pattern, where two candlesticks touch the same bottom or top (depending on its bullish or bearish versions, respectively).

A Technical Note

Given that some important swing trading education elements are advised to be studied in color, I have decided to offer you a FREE electronic copy of this book in **color**.

Please, follow this link to download your color copy:

http://bit.ly/swing-trading-masterclass-oneil

Thank you!

Best,
Kenneth

www.ingramcontent.com/pod-product-compliance
Lightning Source LLC
Chambersburg PA
CBHW020448220526
45464CB00002B/913